OFFERINGS

Remarks on Passing the Plate

ROBERT THAYER

Robert Thayer

SKINNER HOUSE BOOKS
BOSTON

Printed in United States.

Text and cover design by Suzanne Morgan.

ISBN 1-55896-474-6

Library of Congress Cataloging-in-Publication Data

Thayer, Robert A.
    Offerings : remarks on passing the plate/ Robert A. Thayer.
        p. cm.
    ISBN 1-55896-474-6 (alk. paper)
    1. Christian giving—Sermons. 2. Unitarian Universalist
    Association—Sermons. 3. Christian giving—Unitarian
    Universalist Association—Sermons. 4. Sermons, American I.
    Title.
BV772.T44 2004
248'.6—dc22

                                                    2004048184

10 9 8 7 6 5 4 3 2 1
06 05 04

CONTENTS

PREFACE

WHY DO WE STILL PASS THE PLATE? For today's congregations, the drive to fulfill the faith community's mission is primary, so we pass the plate to support our programs and services. But the offering serves another, equally vital function. As part of every worship service, the offering, whether it receives envelopes or the euphemistically termed "loose plate" collection (not to be confused with *loose cannons* or *loose associations*), underscores the message that regular giving is fundamental to the continued and purposeful existence of any faith community.

This small volume is a collection of motivational articles, offertory words, and one song for use by worship leaders in congregations. The offering can be so important, and yet worship leaders have so few resources that fit the occasion. Once you read this book, you may be inspired to mine your own experience in organized religion for similar sermons to deliver before the offering. Most of the material is personal, but this need not hinder its usefulness. Humor and whimsy also play a role in my remarks, as do irony and historical criticism in others. If people can be tickled, why not make them tickled to give?

The motivational pieces grow partly out of worshipping in African-American churches in Mississippi during the voter registration drive of 1964 and later work with Northern AME Zion churches. One simply cannot beat their appeal, called "lifting the offering." The lay leader or the pastor speaks for a good five minutes, determined to bring the Holy Spirit's power upon the people and take them out of worldly selfishness. He or she can inspire parishioners who were reaching for the smallest bill in their wallets to pull out the bigger bills instead.

One goal of this book is to inspire and motivate ministers and lay leaders to write their own sermons for the offering. When you sit down in front of that blank screen or empty notepad, try the following:

~ Search for the part of yourself that prompts you to give. You will find it less awkward to call on the generous hearts of your listeners if you have listened to your own.

~ Learn about the economic and financial realities of your congregation and of religious and non-profit organizations in general. This is a huge field, but the search is worth it. It really helps to talk as if you understand the meaning and power of money.

~ Deliver your message with joy. The act of giving is similar to witnessing the miracle of birth. Your joyful appearance and smile ensure success. Deliver your message with humor as well. Talking about money makes many people uncomfortable; lighten the mood.

~ Connect together stories that become teaching parables. Find stories that neither threaten nor feel alien to peoples' daily lives. Personal testimonies are powerful. Once I asked the moderator of a congregation to get up and say what the church meant to him. He did not realize it, but he was still grieving after losses through death and family reversal. When he spoke, the weight of it all hit him, and this ex-Marine colonel and hard-nosed lawyer broke down in tears. He mumbled as he sat down, "This church means everything to me."

When you face the sometimes awkward task of standing before your faith community and encouraging them to give money, remember that you are speaking *for* the congregation as well as *to* the congregation. Ground yourself in the community's efforts. Remember that your congregation, like a lovely flock of geese, is flying in formation with you at the head of the vee for that moment. Behind you, and honking encouragement, flies the whole flock. The formation knows the route, and shares your direction and your vision.

Robert Thayer
March 2004

WAMPUM

WHEN THE SPANISH CONQUERORS came to the New World after 1492 to claim everything for God and the king and queen of Spain, they brought along a few gold coins. Within months they discovered the source of the gold the Incas and Aztecs mined and crafted to decorate their temples and royal buildings. For the Incas, gold had been nothing more than pretty tinsel, but it was never to be regarded the same way again.

The Spanish enslaved the natives and forced them to mine the gold. They exterminated those who resisted, and converted the survivors to Christianity. The Spanish sent back tons of gold bullion in their galleons to fund the empire's continuing conquest of Europe. The history of gold can make it something of a turn-off as a symbol of value and a medium of exchange. The gifts we each give to our congregation may not be "golden."

The Algonquin Native Americans in southern New England used seashells to craft beads they called *wampum*. They broke off small white shards from conch shells and blue shards from quahog shells and ground them into tubes. It took a full day to make five or six small beads. Then the Algonquins drilled holes in the beads using bone or metal awls, polished the beads, and either strung them lengthwise or fastened them into belts. When a belt was finished, a six-foot wampum belt was a thing of awesome beauty, and its value today would exceed thousands of dollars.

The strung beads or belts of wampum were considered sacred gifts, used for bonding between persons, honoring a leader, and honoring the dead. After 1607, when Dutch trader Adriaen Block landed in southern New England to buy furs, Europeans adopted the native's wampum as real money. The Pequot tribe, in what is present-day Connecticut, quickly monopolized wampum production. Wampum was used by Europeans and natives alike to buy furs, household goods, and land for about a century.

Today the Pequot and other Algonquin tribes attach a degree of sacredness to the wampum belt. A factory-produced belt is not the same as a belt made by hand. Crafting a wampum belt the old-fashioned way is highly labor-intensive, but the result is breath-taking.

Our monetary offering seems more like a belt of wampum than gold, a precious metal with an excessive market value. Our offering signifies what we contribute out of our daily lives, out of our hard work, out of our businesses, trades, crafts, and professions. Like wampum, our offering can also be understood as a form of bonding with one another, honoring our institutions and religious leaders, and respecting our children.

Let us now give and receive what we have crafted and carried here to honor this community.

THE HIGHEST LEVEL

SOMETHING NEEDS to be said every once in a while about reaching our maximum level of giving. In a liberal religious congregation today we know that 15 percent of the donations come in at around $300 every year. While some are giving all that they can reasonably give, we realize that others have the potential to grow in their generosity. In any case, we have learned that reaching the pledge goal depends on our receiving all those $300 contributions!

Gifts from those who are actively involved in the life of the congregation come in at around $1,000 on average per year. Givers at this level view their personal wealth as the fruit of hard work but also as a gift to be managed with stewardship. These folks respond to the mission statement of the congregation as well, because they may have helped to write it or they may see the church's mission as the reason that they belong in the first place.

People that contribute at the highest level (and some even tithe) achieve $2,000 or more per year. Some of these members earn six figures a year, but it is just as likely that they do not, and in fact earn only average household incomes. These people are simply characterized by remarkable generosity.

Once there was a man named John Thayer, who aspired to be in the company of true givers. He was born around 1800 into American Unitarian Christianity and became an ordained minister at a time when Unitarians were giving minimally. In the 1830s, Unitarian Christians took the orthodox Congregationalists to court in Massachusetts and legally wrested their church properties away from them.

Reverend Thayer felt trivialized as a Unitarian, maybe even "corpse cold," as Emerson described his religion. At that time, some Unitarian Christians and Roman Catholics in Massachusetts were working together on social justice issues, and Thayer converted to Catholicism. He was inspired by the French priest Joseph Benedict, who was known for spreading food, clothing, and francs among the poor people of Europe. John Thayer found Benedict's generosity and the power of his example so intense that he became the first Protestant-minister-converted-to-Roman-Catholicism-then-ordained-to-the-priesthood in America. This miracle qualified Father Benedict for canonization!

We North American liberal religionists have now entered the realm of the deeply spiritual. Rich as we are, we may not have "gone through the eye of the needle," but we have certainly produced mega-givers since Father Thayer left us. So if you are one or would be one, you are in good company.

A FREE CHURCH

Ours is a free church, but it is not free. The offering portion of our worship service is a reminder of what it means to support our own religious community instead of having somebody else support it and tell us how to live and where to go if we dissent and disobey. The offering reminds us that our congregation belongs to us, to each of us, as well as to the whole of us.

Our worship includes a sung invitation to "enter, rejoice, and come in." Enter, and bring your mind and full heart with you. Rejoice, and know that the sadness and mourning we all go through teaches us why and how to rejoice. Come in, and bring your commitment with you in the form of a pledge or a contribution. Let our offering be a way to our commitment real and public.

Jesus taught his disciples, "If you go to the temple and there remember that your brother or sister has aught against you, leave your gift on the altar, and first go, and be reconciled with your brother or sister. Then return and make your gift at the altar." Let this spiritual direction remain uppermost in our minds. Let us give as we live in balance and harmony with our people.

5

The Hebrew prophets of Yahweh were skeptical of the temple-based religion in Jerusalem, with its hereditary priesthood and its royal Davidic connection. Micah taught that God requires one thing of the gathered congregation—not burnt offerings, not offerings of valuables, and not one's first-born child—"but to do justly and love mercy and walk humbly with your God." That is the timeless and still relevant prophetic shift. As we also walk in the Abrahamic tradition, we walk together humbly and share the real financial burdens for bringing justice and mercy to our world, and we know that God, or whatever we call the ultimate, wants only this.

In the 1970s many spiritual searchers found the book *Be Here Now*. The author, Ram Dass, once remarked, "When a pickpocket sees a holy person, he sees only the guru's pockets." In other words, the pickpocket always misses the spiritual point. Perhaps a few of us have had the weird sense that some gurus and religions will pick your pockets and care nothing for your spiritual growth. In our beloved community we do not look at one another's pockets. We look into each other's faces and see the same longing, pain, and fulfillment that lie in our own. Our offering grows out of the mystery and wonder of looking into one another's souls.

THE LAST DOLLAR

ONE MONDAY MORNING I got a telephone call at home from a friend who was a self-employed shipwright. He was divorced with a grown son and a regular at Sunday worship. The conversation went like this:

"Bob, you will never believe what happened to me yesterday in church and this morning."

"Well, Norm, I'm all ears."

"Remember the offering? You said, 'This is a free church, but it is not free' and you asked us to give as we're able to keep the church free."

"Right," I replied.

"Well, wouldn't you know it?" Norm began, "I reached into my wallet and saw one dollar, my last dollar. I don't have a job right now and have applied at all the shipyards."

"Norm, I think I can understand the angst of that moment."

"'Well,' I thought to myself," he went on, "'Here is the minister asking for an offering, and I have exactly one dollar left to my name.' I hesitated a second and thought, 'Oh, what the heck, give it up.' And I did just that, but with a prayer that since I was now completely broke, God would come across with at least a lead for a job."

"Okay," I replied, feeling bad all of a sudden because Norm was entering a realm of spiritual discipline that I had not taught or encouraged.

"Later I went to my sister's for Sunday dinner," Norm continued, "and I never said a word about it. Then I went home and tried to sleep. At 8:00 AM on the button, a man I never heard of called me and said, 'Are you Norm, the shipwright?' And I said, 'Yes, what can I do for you?' He said, 'I have a 1923 antique motor craft that needs restoring. Can you do it?'"

Norm went on, "So I'm ready to leave, but the gas gauge in my truck indicates that I don't have enough gas to get to his place, so I have to go to my sister's and borrow eight dollars. Bob, I think I may have five months of work to do for him. I can't tell you what it feels like right now."

"Norm, what can I say, except how glad I am for your break? But do you really think there is a connection? Isn't it just a coincidence?"

"Well, I was hoping you might clarify that for me. You see, I really did pray for a job. So I wondered, did God hear my prayer or what?"

"Norm, just go," I said. "I will forever cherish your dollar in the plate."

"Okay, Bob. I'm out the door."

Friends, you may be down to your last dollar. But if you truly wish it, you can become detached from the power of money and give the dollar away. Your life will never be the same afterward.

LARGE BILLS

SOME YEARS AGO I visited England and attended Sunday worship with some British Unitarian friends. We sat toward the front of the church. I was all tingly—both from the cold sanctuary and the warm glow of being on my ancestral soil. The sermon was magnificent, and I was feeling effusive, very generous.

The moment came for the offering. I reached into my wallet and saw a wad of British pound notes, but nothing particularly small. I mentally shrugged my shoulders and pulled out a twenty-pound note, held it in my hand, and prepared to drop it in. My friend shook his head at me. I raised my eyebrows at him—why not? He whispered, "It's a rather large donation."

I felt indignant. Who was my friend to tell me I was giving too much. I flapped the twenty-pound note in the air and whispered, "Are you sure?"

"See the usher?" he asked. "I know he will be in shock. He may fall down. He has never seen a twenty-pound note in a collection except for famine relief in India."

"Now you have me curious. Let's see if you are right," I responded testily.

"Be mindful," he warned, "that this usher will ask you after the service if you would like change."

Well, it did not happen that way. When I dropped the note in the plate, the usher initially reacted with a frown, but his face soon brightened with a proper smile. Then I realized something very thrilling. Because we sat in front, every British Unitarian on our side of the aisle that morning would see that note in the plate. What an example, I thought. On second thought, I remembered that since World War II the Brits have had a thorough familiarity with Yanks and many think of us as "oversexed, over-paid, and over here."

At the end of the service, I shook hands with people all around me, including the usher, and gave hugs to my two colleagues who had been in the pulpit that day. After we walked out into the chill October morning, I looked back into the vestibule and saw the usher take out my note. He looked outside down the walkway, caught my eye, and said, "Thank you very much."

Some days you may come to church with only large bills, and even if you make your pledge payment faithfully by mail, you may wonder, what can I give today? Let the spirit guide you. I can only say that the one time I surprised the British usher, I felt the thrill of pure joy that only giving money can bring. May you have pure joy in the moment when we give and receive our offering.

THE MAN WHO FORGOT

In 1961 I was a newly ordained pastor serving a congregation of Presbyterians, and one Sunday a man named MacKinnon got up from his pew, left his wife, and slowly walked out the center aisle and disappeared out the back of the church.

After worship ended I approached a lay leader and inquired why MacKinnon had left. "Was he taken ill with something?" I asked.

"No," answered the leader. "He just forgot his offering envelope and went home to get it. And if I were you, I would say nothing to him about it. He is not one of our biggest givers, but what he contributes is loyal support."

"But walking out of church in the middle of things is extreme, it seems to me. Why not wait? What's the big deal?" I asked.

"His wife stayed. That says a lot," was the reply.

Some weeks later I screwed up my courage and approached MacKinnon after worship. I told him what the lay leader had said and added, "I appreciate how seriously you take your offering, how important it is to you."

"You want to know the real story?" he volunteered.

"I'd be happy to hear it," I said.

"My wife sent me out of church that day to get the offering because she does the finances in our house. She had handed the envelope to me to bring, and I left it on the dresser. She said, 'One of us is going back. Which will it be?'"

"I'm just learning about the people in the congregation, and you've helped me understand things," I said.

"The rest is better left unsaid, I suppose, but you might as well know that I'm not a very good churchgoer. I come because she insists, and that's okay. She does things for me that I know she's not devoted to. But the pledge money is entirely her choice, and when I forgot it, I let her down. I would never live it down if I left that envelope at home."

"I guess it's the way she was raised, am I right?" I ventured further.

"That you are. She was raised to come to church with the offering or else stay home." Then MacKinnon smiled and tossed his head back and laughed a little. "You know the Scots," he said, "tight-fisted, but when they give their hard-earned money away, it's like a bolt of lightning coming down from heaven."

When the time comes for the offering on Sunday morning, please do not walk out if you came without your pledge or without your wallet. Stay with us. We love you. I know you are not tight-fisted. But keep watch when you pass the plate in the pew. Someone's gift may cause a flash of lightening. The plates are not grounded, and it could be a hot time.

THE OFFERING ENABLER

I WAS ELEVEN YEARS OLD. It was a Sunday in the summertime in Charleston, West Virginia, and the family was all in church, where Mother sang in the choir. The women took off their dresses in a choir room and put on robes over their slips. Most of them carried their pocketbooks as they filed into the choir stall, but Mother had tucked her offering envelope down the front of her slip.

During the sermon the second soprano next to Mom dosed off. The kindly minister's sermons were enough to tranquilize a hungry tiger. The second soprano had idly diddled one of her fingers into the molding on the back of the choir rail, and it got stuck in the hole.

As the usher came into the choir stall to take the collection, I noticed that my mother was crouched in a clearly uncontrolled fit of laugher. (This was not all that unusual.) The second soprano had evidently dropped her pocketbook with her offering envelope, and mother crouched down to pick it up, got out the woman's envelope, and dropped it in the usher's plate. However, the usher was embarrassed and left the choir stall before Mother could drop in our family's offering.

When the choir rose to lead in the singing of the Doxology, the second soprano was still unable to stand because of her stuck finger. As worship closed, Mother managed to stand erect in her place and sing the closing hymn, but after the benediction, she collapsed in silent laughter next to the second soprano.

After the worship ended, the second soprano managed to get the attention of one of the men. He went into the supply closet and brought back a screwdriver, unscrewed the roundhead brass screws holding the wooden molding, and took the woman to the fellowship hall. There he found a small coping saw and surgically removed the wooden molding from the woman's finger.

Mother watched the surgical removal from a nearby chair, and she was laughing so hard that people came to find out what the ruckus was. The usher came to Mother and asked if she had forgotten her offering envelope. Mother screamed in a paroxysm of giddy laughter, reached into her bodice (I believe that is the gracious term), and pulled out her offering envelope.

A staunch supporter of that congregation, Mother taught me the value of making a weekly contribution. This time she put the second soprano's offering before her own and helped the offering to take place.

When the collection plate comes around during the worship service, please wake your neighbor and make sure he or she drops the offering into the plate before you drop yours in. And if your neighbor has his or her finger stuck in any kind of decorative molding, hang in there. Perhaps the sexton keeps a coping saw in the closet.

RELIGION AND PATRIOTISM

I MARVEL AT THE religious freedom and freedom of opportunity for religion in this nation. Granted, some of the religions that grow and prosper give me moments of uneasiness. That aside, we should know how vital it is to our freedom not to have a religious organization, buildings and all, paid for with our tax money.

Before 1787 most New England towns had parish churches that were supported by taxes. In fact, in 1775, two laymen, founders of the historic First Baptist church in Medfield, Massachusetts, were sentenced to two years in jail for not paying taxes to support the town's Congregational church, First Parish. Many members of First Parish can trace their family's membership in the church back over several generations, but the story of these two dissenters remains largely untold.

The true meaning of the offering we give and receive every worship day is that we affirm one of the greatest negatives in the world: There is no state church here. We affirm the positive, that with each dollar we give, we keep the Revolution alive, and we support our own Association's right to grow and prosper.

The Revolution stalled, however, in 1787. The Constitution left slavery in place and defined a black person as three-fifths of a white male. African-American slaves were prohibited from worshipping freely in the South until April 1865, when General Robert E. Lee surrendered to General Ulysses S. Grant at Appomattox Court House. Only then did the power of the African-American Christian churches rise like a new mountain range throughout the Southern landscape.

Our Revolution is never over. Year after year some bill gets tagged onto legislation in Congress to pay for one more educational service provided by a religion that owns its own schools. Every time our offering is passed, I think of the hymn that goes, "O, freedom. O, freedom. O freedom over me." Be free. Give generously.

THE CONGREGATIONAL STORY

ALTHOUGH THE AMERICAN Revolution won for all the right to freedom of worship, we should remember that there is another kind of religious freedom, one that is directly supported by the contributions of a faith community's members. This liberty is still relatively new, and not universal. It is freedom from your local congregation's old oligarchy, the few well-off and controlling families. If you look back into the history and legacy of denominational families that go back three, four, maybe five generations, the untold story is that those families controlled the local congregations. Of course, the rental of pews, even the owning of pews in some cases, constituted the chief means of support before 1920. The oligarchy can be interpreted in two ways. Perhaps the leading families so loved their congregations and ministers that when the annual contributions or the rentals fell short of the hoped-for goal, the wealthier families made up the entire difference. Or perhaps the leading families loved their congregations and ministers and paid for the main expenses because they wanted everything that was said and done to suit their tastes.

Either way, there was not much freedom of the pulpit, as some activist clergy found out when they participated in civil rights and antiwar movements; they drew intense criticism from a few powerful families and were eased off their career ladders.

Since the Unitarian Universalist Association instituted the Every Member Canvass in the 1960s and 1970s and modified it over the decades, congregation members have found themselves with more prerogatives and decision-making power. Everyone "pays the piper and calls the tune."

So remember that your offering supports the democratic process, the right of conscience, and a new congregational story—of how generous support is offered by and received by each member of the community.

A PENNY MORE OR LESS

AMERICAN NOVELIST William Faulkner, who won the Nobel Prize for Literature in 1949, gave an acceptance speech in which he said, "I believe that Man will not merely endure: Man will prevail. Man is immortal, not because he alone has an inexhaustible voice, but because he has a soul, a spirit capable of compassion and sacrifice and endurance." Of course, today we would say "humanity" or "human beings" rather than "man." Compassion, sacrifice, and endurance: These are the virtues that form the basis of our liberal religion, and other religions as well.

In his short story "A Rose for Emily," Faulkner writes about money: "When her father died, it got about that the house was all that was left to her; and in a way, people were glad. At last they could pity Miss Emily. Being left alone, and a pauper, she had become humanized. Now she too would know the old thrill and the old despair of a penny more or less."

When I stumbled across these lines, my first wife and I were in seminary in Chicago and living from hand to mouth with our one-year-old daughter. We wondered why we were so poor in our twenties. We knew it could be worse; we could be denied our human rights like African Americans. But still, that phrase really hit me, "a penny more or less." Whenever our parents sent small care packages, our spirits soared.

Being human is both the great glory and the great leveler of our lives on the earth. The glory is well expressed by Faulkner's "compassion and sacrifice and endurance." The great leveler, "the old thrill and the old despair of a penny more or less."

When we pass the offering plate, we need to be sensitive to the fact that everyone is on the same level, really, and we all know the old thrill and the old despair. And just as each person knows it, so does each congregation know the old thrill and the old despair of an increase and a shortfall. Some congregations have raised endowments in order to make the annual budget less of a roller-coaster ride.

We can acknowledge that we are human and that we have all the feelings that go with that. Let us give and receive our offering every Sunday in the light of the reality that every penny more that you give brings that old thrill to the treasurer and to the entire membership of your beloved faith community.

THE MARK OF SCARCITY

WE WHO GREW UP in or lived through the Great
Depression wear a "mark of scarcity." Even if we
belonged to a well-off family, we shared the school-
rooms, streets, buses, and dime-store counters with des-
perate people. I cannot forget the many young children
who came to my school unbathed, without shoes on
their feet, with colds and fevers, and dressed in rags.

Our family went to church often during the
Depression and the Second World War. At one church
supper in September 1945, I watched a remarkable sight,
a ceremony to mark the final payment on the church
mortgage. At the head table stood a cast-iron kettle, sur-
rounded by two elders of the church and the minister.
Thirty years had gone by since 1915, when the new building went up. Mother was a child of eight at the time and
was later admitted to the Lord's Supper, or received into
full membership. I saw her and my grandmother crying.
My dad sat there stoically. The two elders, who had helped
to secure the mortgage, spoke words of congratulations.
The minister gave thanks to God in a very long prayer.
Then as one elder held up the bank note, the other lit a

match and set it on fire. The flames were bright. The flaming document was dropped into the kettle. We closed by singing hymns. I had a falsetto voice and sang loudly.

The next year I witnessed another exciting program. After the church supper there was a debate between the minister and an elder, a local coal-mine owner. The issue was whether to borrow money to build a new addition onto the church so that we could have a larger Sunday School and attract more members. The minister took the aye side, while the mine owner took the nay side.

The debate went on for about a half hour. Then the elders took a paper-ballot vote, and the results were something like twenty ayes and forty nays. The minister lost. On the ride back home I asked Mom and Dad how they voted. They told me they voted aye with the minister, who had performed their wedding, officiated at the funeral of Mom's father, baptized me and my brothers, and mentored me to admission to the Lord's Supper.

"So why do you think he lost the debate?" I asked. "And why did you vote aye?"

"Everyone remembers the Depression, and most are worried that those days will come again," explained my father. "And he made strong points: The Depression is over; we need to act now for the future of the church and to trust God as we always trust God."

When the collection plate is passed, let those of us who wear the mark of scarcity join with those whose good fortune it was to never wear the mark, and celebrate a virtual burning of that mark with an overflowing offering of plenty.

THE MAN IN THE BALCONY

THE ACADEMIC YEAR was 1958-1959. I was enrolled in seminary and working as an intern for a midsize Protestant congregation in Chicago. My assignment was to assist in Sunday worship and to lead two youth programs. At noon most Sundays I joined the pastor and his family for dinner. One Sunday he told me that a new man had been attending worship since the fall, and each Sunday he was putting a twenty-dollar bill into the offering plate. He sat in the balcony. My pastor described him, and I remembered who he was.

"Does anybody know who he is or anything about his family? Does he have kids?" I inquired.

"The grapevine has it," the pastor said, "that he owns a business in Chicago."

"I am just learning here," I volunteered, "but would it be proper procedure to pay him a pastoral visit?"

"Our head deacon has asked the man," the pastor replied, "and the deacon reports that he might like a call later, but he did not say when."

"Wow," I blurted out. "Isn't twenty dollars a week a small fortune? Does anyone else give that much?"

Before I finish this story, I can tell you that in today's dollars, that man's weekly donation would exceed $200. So we can appreciate the usher's astonishment when the man's offering kept on coming.

"No," replied the pastor, "and we're perplexed. Do they talk about this sort of thing in seminary today? It's been ten years since I graduated."

"Not that I've ever heard," I answered.

"Well, in casual conversation, he indicated that you were the main reason he attends. He gets a great deal out of the way you read scripture and offer prayer."

The pastor smiled at me, as did his wife. He had been an Army chaplain in Korea for two years and also, I gathered, a missionary there for several more years, and he carried within him that compassion and composure I had seen in returning missionaries.

Then his face grew serious. He glanced at his wife. "I have been told by a certain deacon that this man wants you to become the minister here when you are ordained."

"Uh oh," I said. "Does he want me to replace you?"

"That would be in at least two years, I think," the pastor said. "I might have moved on by then, but not likely. I am not swayed by this offer—or demand, if that is what he is making—but I think you should know and take it for what it is worth: experience."

"I think I can say," I declared without giving it a second thought and using the quote from the gospel, "'No person can serve two masters. He/she will hate the one and love the other. You cannot serve God and money.'"

Contributing to the offering every week means that the largest donor does not decide the ministry in your congregation. But by all means, leave $200 in the offering if your conscience dictates such a gift. You will be loved and, unlike the man in the balcony, trusted.

ENDOWMENTVILLE

THE PROBLEM IN CERTAIN congregations with large endowments is that it is very easy to neglect regular contribution, depending on the endowment to carry the congregation along. The tune for the following song is "Margaritaville" by Jimmy Buffett.

Livin' on kale soup, trying to regroup,
Starting the luncheon now that we've prayed.
Sippin' our coffee, in the committee,
All of us asking if staff will be paid.

> Chorus:
> Coastin' along again on our endowment,
> Searching for our last market report,
> Some people claim the UUA is to blame,
> But I know, it's nobody's fault.

A holistic wonder, with mystical thunder,
We knew our preacher could fill every pew.
But church-goers join up, and then they get fed up,
And why they leave we haven't a clue.

    Coastin' along again on our endowment,
    Searching for our last market report.
    Some people claim the UUA is to blame,
    But I think, well, it could be our fault.

The rain is still falling, the roof is still leaking.
Hurricanes come and we might have known.
But we have investments and soon they will net us
A cool hundred thousand to help us hang on.

    Coastin' along again on our endowment,
    Searching for our last market report.
    Some people claim the UUA is to blame,
    But I know, it's our own darn fault.

A CHEERFUL GIVER

THE RECORDS OF THE early Christian community do not provide many models for twenty-first–century congregations. There is one passage in the Apostle Paul's letters, however, that has to do with giving money and has endured to this day. In the context of Paul's one fundraising effort of his missionary work among the new Hellenistic churches, Paul writes, "The Lord loves a cheerful giver." As part of his appeal, Paul says that his mission is to relieve the poverty of the Jewish Christians in Palestine.

One negative interpretation of this campaign, supported by A. Powell Davies, says that Paul raised money intending to buy respect for himself and gentile congregations. But it is possible that Jewish Christians experienced a true fiscal crisis caused by their experiment with communal living. In Palestine, the first baptized Christians gave up their own vocations, sold their property and their personal possessions, and turned the proceeds over to the church. Then everyone subsisted on the ecclesiastical treasury (*ecclesia* is the Greek word for "church"). They did this in order to be prepared for the rapture of the immediate Second Coming of Jesus.

Paul's appeal went out to the new churches in Hellenistic cities. Here the believers did not practice communal living, so they could generate funds from their own occupations. Paul urged them, "Each should give not grudgingly or of necessity, but willingly, for the Lord loves a cheerful giver." That is the sentence that has survived to our time. Perhaps these early Christians were able to give cheerfully because they got to keep everything they made. We need only to think of the joy that everyone in Communist Eastern Europe felt when the Berlin wall came down to understand. And perhaps they were cheerful because they felt prosperous; they did not have to worry about the roof over their heads or about daily rations of food and wine. But a third reason for their cheer might be the Lord's love that Paul spoke of. That may not warm many liberal religious hearts because many of us no longer believe in the *Lord*. So the question is: What or who gives us love when we give cheerfully? Although we don't know the answer, we *feel* loved when we give, and we know self-love and self-respect when we give, but the source of that love remains a mystery.

Let us feel the cheer that comes from being a free people with unparalleled worldly goods and accept the mystery that in the spiritual life, at least, we humans do cheerfully turn from taking to giving.

THE WIDOW'S MITE

THE ONE FIRST-CENTURY Jerusalem temple practice that three of the four Gospel writers described without disapproval concerns the offering taken daily by the temple priesthood. The priests did not pass the plate, but they kept an offering box, called the treasury, at the outer door of the sanctuary. Each individual who entered for prayer or sacrifice or holy days was obliged to make a contribution.

We pick up the story with Jesus and the twelve disciples standing outside the temple one day across from the treasury, with Jesus trying to impart to them his own sense of the spiritual discipline around giving. One by one people entered and put in their money. Several rich persons entered and made their offerings, followed by a certain widow. She dropped in a penny, a nothing, a mite, as it was translated in the King James Bible. Jesus' teaching went something like this: "The others going in today gave out of their abundance, but the widow gave out of her poverty, and she gave more than anybody else."

New members in the congregation usually ask, "How much do people contribute? What is expected of us?" The answer comes back: "You give at your best possible level (suggesting 2.5 percent of income as a goal) to enable the congregation to carry out its mission and support its annual budget."

We almost never make the point that Jesus made in speaking to his disciples, that is that we owe praise to the widow's mite and the proportionate size of her contribution. Her contribution was a hardship. She may have cut herself short for the week. She may not be able to make her credit-card minimum payment or buy her grandchild's birthday present. We need to think not of a person's exact amount, but the proportion and what that proportion costs. If your family makes over $100,000 a year, a $2,000 contribution will not kill you. If you are barely making ends meet on $9 an hour, even a dollar a week could hurt. The poor individual who is already getting "nickeled and dimed to death" and puts in a dollar a week gives more than you and I do when we put in $50 a week.

Let us honor and give kudos to those among us who find that whatever they contribute to the congregation, this gift comes out of flesh and blood, and it is dear. We now know how truly large such a gift is and how blessed this congregation is to have some very generous members.

ALL THAT I HAVE IS YOURS

THE FOLLOWING WAS once a common saying in mainstream Protestant churches: "God gives us everything we have; therefore, as we give to others, we are only giving back what belongs to God." Hymns from the sixteenth through twentieth centuries often made this admonition in bold terms. Martin Luther's hymn "A Mighty Fortress Is Our God" even goes so far as to say, "Let goods and kindred go. . . ."

Many reverent Protestants sing those words with enthusiasm and do not mean them for a moment. What person in his/her right mind believes their kindred are expendable? Well, there is something more to be said.

The metaphor of "giving back" everything holds meaning when one stops to consider that the Creator "takes back" our lives at the moment of our deaths. As Rabindranath Tagore writes, "I give the whole and not the part of all you gave to me; my goods, my life, my soul, my heart, I yield them all to thee." This notion grows out of our sense of being mortal and yet having the power to make great decisions. In a moment of great personal insight, Unitarian Universalist minister Forrest

Church said, "Religion is what you do with your life once you realize you are going to die." When you and I cross this path of light, we can begin to let go of our beings. We consider how much difference we can make with a bequest here and a living trust somewhere else.

It's not that our estate belongs to God; it's just that you have power to yield it up in a way that can mend one broken heart, help one robin back into her nest, to paraphrase Emily Dickinson. Know for a fact that one day you may make a huge difference in the world you shall leave and that the offering you make is but a small token of your true power.

GIVING TO THE DISASTER

STORIES ABOUT GENEROUS HEARTS are not hard to find. People give after any disaster. Money poured into the New York City relief funds after terrorists flew the planes into the Twin Towers and the Pentagon and killed three thousand people. Your own congregation may see the day when it must send out a disaster appeal.

When it comes to routine giving to a congregation, the members are asked to respond to the community's mission. For some members, this "mission" language can seem like a secret code. One couple who joined a church in 1967, where no person-to-person appeal was ever addressed to them, were confused about their annual pledge. The husband and wife decided to pledge 5 percent of their income, based on an article they had read in our denomination's magazine. They had never made this kind of stretch before, but the article stated that with their income level, giving between 2.5 percent and 5 percent was reasonable if the church was to fulfill its mission.

At their first annual church meeting, the couple heard the humble, modest committee reports typical of small congregations, and the treasurer's report covered every iota of income and expenditure. The pledge drive raised $11,000 from sixty families. Of this total, the couple had given $600! On the sheet that broke down the pledge groups, theirs was three times the next highest pledge! They had come in from the secular cold to provide a spiritual grounding for their three kids, only to find that their church was a deadbeat. Disappointed but true to their word, the couple paid their pledge. The next year they cut it in half, but it was still the highest. I came on board as the minister in the midst of this slippery slope. Each annual drive fell off from the previous years. In their fourth year, as a result of this and other disappointments, the couple left the congregation.

After we lost this prize family, disaster struck: an empty treasury, an unpaid minister and organist, unpaid laborers repairing the roof, rampant vandalism to the building, frozen and broken water pipes, and a terrible if unrelated disaster—the murder of a young man by a mob outside the back door of the vestry one winter night.

The Board called a special meeting. Fifty-five members attended. On a hot July Sunday, the motion to fire the minister lost 52 to 0, with three abstentions. Then the president asked for a new commitment from everybody. The money raised that afternoon refunded the budget. Staff was paid. Repairs were funded. Out of disaster came the mission: to be a real congregation.

We must always remember one thing: If we contribute generously and regularly, it will keep disaster at bay. Giving to a mission is cleaner, better, nicer, and more efficient than the thrill of repairing any disaster.

IT'S NOT JUST YOUR FAVORITE
CHARITY ANY MORE

—————————

PEOPLE BELONGING TO THE generation born between 1900 and 1922 were known to give their money consistently to a single nonprofit, their "favorite charity." The "favorite charity" concept helped to build the infrastructures of Protestant, Catholic, and Jewish colleges, seminaries, and service organizations in North America.

Today's U.S. taxpayers contribute perhaps 6 percent of the Gross Domestic Product, and much of that total goes to religious institutions. But the giving pattern for individuals is much wider now. One member of my family, who contributes to her religious institution, gives all she can possibly afford to programs for young people living on Native American reservations.

A person I'll call Eleanor chose two institutions to support with her time and money: her faith community and a maritime museum that held great significance for her. She pledged each year to her church's annual drive at the highest level in the congregation, and contributed her time generously as well. At the same time, she donated 30,000 hours of volunteer time to the maritime museum, which she also remembered in her will. Eleanor did not need to seek gainful employment, but she knew she had to follow a path of meaningful service or else wilt on the vine. She pitched in to make a better world by serving in two places.

Don't look now, but your congregation includes its own marathon donors, who give to several causes. Far ahead of the pack in their giving, they will always win the gold and wear the laurel crown in our memories. But they never do this to put us to shame. They are out there to inspire us.

A MOTHER'S OBJECTION

THIS IS ABOUT THE lesson my mother, who was an accountant and business manager before marrying my father, tried to impress upon me, with limited results. When I told my folks I felt called to the ministry and was about to apply to divinity school, my mother told me I was making a big mistake, that I was about to give my life away, that I would never be paid what I was worth, and that in fact, "If you ever fall in love and marry, you will be unable to provide for your family."

She told me what the salary package was for our beloved minister at the time, who was married and the father of four grown children and served one of the wealthiest congregations in the state. My reaction was rather stoic, I think. My mother began to rant and told me, "If that church had any decency, they would double his package tomorrow, and I know they could."

After I got married I went off to seminary, and to make sure I had no worries, my parents paid all the expenses of the first year. The second year we got by on our own, and the third year I earned sufficient scholarship money to make ends meet.

Upon graduation my parents urged me to give up ministry. We refused. We were called to our first settlement and moved into the parsonage. All went well at first. After a couple of years and two babies, true to Mother's prediction, we were having money problems. As Mother and Father cursed organized religion (not for its beliefs, but for its salaries), they gave us a gift of stock to underwrite our family.

When the 1970s hit us with several small recessions and sticky religious controversies that kept promotions for me out of reach, we were insolvent. After the birth of our third child, I opted for an institutional chaplaincy that paid fairly well, and my wife went into elementary teaching.

We were out of the woods. Mother stopped chiding me for wasting my life. She and Father valued my ministry and encouraged me. When my parents died, they left me a little money, which seemed like a fortune to us. Belatedly, I was inspired by my mother's values to speak out for my professional package, without anger or guilt, and to insist that high standards be met.

Please know that a portion of your offering goes to support the ordained minister. With pride in this profession and with no false modesty, we affirm that the ordained leaders are worth every dollar of it.

If financial support is kept at the highest level, we heap good fortune on ourselves and the ministers' families, and if not, the opposite applies. The "living tradition" of ministry is an ancient path. People will never stop walking that path, and it is an act of spiritual enlightenment for congregations to meet their worldly needs.

THE PRIME SCOLDER

ONCE I ATTENDED a pledge campaign dinner in a historic church. The Pledge Committee arranged an after-dinner program of short skits to loosen up the mood and inspire the giving. One skit featured a woman dressed in a 1940s costume. She portrayed an overbearing person with an authoritative look and tone to her voice. She raised her finger and wagged it, then pointed at all of us seated at the supper. She began:

All you good people out there have been coming to this church for quite a while and have benefited in many ways from your regular attendance. And we have not seen some of you here tonight in many months. You should be ashamed of yourselves for ignoring your duty.

Well, I won't waste words on the obvious. I have been asked to state the case for contributing to our finances. We need your contribution. As this is a democracy, just like the town we live in, we have to raise money or we cannot continue to exist. We must go through this tiresome rigamarole every year, but as the great founding father Ben Franklin once said, "It's a democracy, madam, if you can keep it." Consider the alternative, in our case, a state church.

I come to this parish out of ten generations and every one of those generations supported this congregation. It is in our blood, as the saying goes. But I see that it is not in everybody's blood, and that creates a disappointment in some of us. Many of you can well afford to give more but do not. If this congregation is not in your blood, you should think seriously about how to get it into your blood.

You've heard the saying, "Give until it hurts." I say, give because it hurts. If you do not feel it, you are not really giving at all; you are just playing at giving, like a child playing doctor, pretending to take out an appendix. Some of you are doing this here. Stop playing doctor and start acting real!

Thank you for listening to me. I know that people normally cannot bear to have me talk in public for very long. They tell me it wears on them. Well, I have worn on you all I care to, so I'm through.

When the actress finished her monologue, she sat down to a rousing wave of laughter and applause. The pledge results that evening reached the target set by the Board and exceeded it.

We gave up scolding many years ago. But her satire illustrates a path we once took and now avoid. Our appeal is to your heart and mind and we add to your generosity. And may peace be with you.

A FORMAL CEREMONY WITH GLOVES

LET US ACKNOWLEDGE that the weekly offering we take has inherent worth, to borrow a familiar phrase. Therefore, it does not do much good (and it can be risky) to try to enhance its worth by making the collection a formal occasion.

I heard a story on this subject from a delegate I met at a General Assembly. When we had introduced ourselves to each other and identified our congregations, he told me that he had attended my New England church when he was in the Navy in World War II and stationed nearby.

"I would see the male ushers," he began, "dressed in dark suits and ties. On cue, the head usher would go to a table at the rear of the sanctuary, take out these gray gloves, and hand a pair to each of the ushers. They put on the gloves and then lined up at the rear of the church, like sailors on deck.

"After the minister announced the offering, the ushers marched in twos to the front of the church. The aisle was long. The sight of men marching in step was pretty impressive. Each had a kind of somber expression.

"But on one Sunday morning when the ushers came to the front and stopped, they did not turn, split up, and take the offering. They remained in formation.

"The head usher stared at the communion table, which normally held the silver offering plates, and saw that the table was bare. He marched forward beyond the communion table to the pulpit platform and searched for the plates there. But no plates were to be seen.

"Then he did a right-face and marched back to the formation. With a nod from this head usher, the other five ushers did an about-face. The two trailing ushers, now in the lead of the column, stepped off and led a recessional march to the rear of the church.

"During their recessional, the organist, who was out of sight in the choir loft, went ahead and played the offertory to accompany the untaken collection. After finishing that, he played the Doxology. When the congregation rose and sang 'All people that on earth do dwell…' the ushers were spread out stiff and expressionless along the back wall.

"Then the minister bowed his head, said the offertory prayer, and sat down. Not one word was said about the offering. Someone had forgotten to go to the safe, work the combination, and remove the plates."

The old salt, then in his seventies, concluded, "I'll never forget that service or that church, ever." What he meant exactly, I will never know.

Whatever be the lessons learned over the years since World War II, one is that we have to have the plates or baskets to pass. We probably do have gray gloves somewhere, but they would not add much. We no longer march in step. We no longer wear dark suits and ties. But we have made a significant change: We have women taking the offering now. And they would ask, "Where are the plates?"

A TRANSCENDENTAL OFFERING
WITH YOUTH IN MIND

———————————

YEARS AGO, I ASKED a scholar in American church history, "What has been the main good that the children and followers of the liberal religious wing of Protestant congregations have brought to America? What's been their main contribution?" His answer: "The Transcendentalists and other movements that are linear descendants, the abolitionists and women's suffrage organizers."

In one way the Transcendentalists did what the Founding Fathers did: They wrote a spiritual/ethical constitution for human fulfillment. They created models for balanced living, calls to social justice for all humanity, teachings on spiritual search and growth, and guides for encountering world religions. This is still what Americans need to learn.

People should know that Emerson and the other Transcendentalists in New England, with one exception, opted out of their own Unitarian congregations. Most began as children or friends of this faith community. The pattern with many spiritually innovative individuals from European and American faiths is that the religions they grow in and first serve cannot understand them, but those same religions proudly claim them years later.

Transcendentalist Fredrick Henry Hedge of Portland, Maine, remained active in the ministry, and one of the gifts he left was that he introduced us to German idealists and romantics at a time when many Unitarians were limited to British religious concepts. He translated Luther's "A Mighty Fortress Is Our God" into an English version that is still in use today.

In our own time, we impart some pretty dynamic values to our youth, and we hope that they may someday fashion a body of wisdom and behavior that we can barely imagine. In their spiritual lives they may transcend our nurture of them and move beyond us, but at this moment in time, our offering is for them and their future witness.

A MESSAGE FROM CADES COVE, TENNESSEE

EVERY YEAR THE TOWN of Cades Cove, located in the heart of the Great Smoky Mountain National Park, is host to five million tourists who wend their way by motor vehicle around the one-lane circular road to view what still stands of the homes, barns, and churches there. Cades Cove was a small farming community founded in 1820. Its residents were forced to move out when it became part of the National Park in 1927, but the history and legends of the place are beguiling. Cades Cove existed on land that once belonged to the Cherokee and was unethically taken from them. The most rending conflict in Cades Cove occurred during the Civil War, when half of the population of maybe eight hundred rejected the Confederacy and sided with the Union and the antislavery cause.

Cades Cove inhabitants grew several Protestant congregations for their "nourishment unto salvation," and the Primitive Baptist Church was the spiritual home of many of the town's political leaders and religious leaders. Except for the cost of erecting the building, there was virtually no expense to running the church year-in and year-out. The ministers were chosen and ordained by the regional district, and they never got a penny except for conducting occasional funerals.

The culture of Cades Cove involved a continuous form of contribution within each church and among all the residents, which served to maintain a family's material position if that family fell on hard times. Death, fire, accident, illness, abandonment—the church members had a duty to see that the family wanted for nothing. Often they even took over all the farm duties. The records of Cades Cove show the people's total compliance, documenting a pattern of survival for each stricken family for over a century.

Many of us who have been at church work for decades have often wished we gave less money to our institutional religion and more to those in need at our doorstep and around the globe. When an urban riot rips apart a city, a famine hits a flood-ravaged delta or AIDS infects half a country in Africa, some would like to sell the pews and stained glass for humanitarian relief.

Let us take heart that in both our worship and polity, we do not ignore the sufferings of any human being. In this religious community, we talk about others' sufferings, just as we talk about our own. The offering is a way of asking our community one basic question: How does our contribution position us today, and tomorrow, to alleviate another's suffering?

DIFFERENT WAYS
TO COUNT THE GIVING

WHEN A CERTAIN CONGREGATION conducted its first "every member" pledge drive in 1972, the Board and the Finance Committee believed they were taking a leap forward in responsible government. In this congregation there were some new families that the old members counted on to help out. One family in particular—a man, a woman, and three children—was new to the denomination as well, and when the canvasser called, they wrote down a pledge of $500, not knowing exactly how they would pay it.

The family made the same pledge year after year, but a small scandal developed when the Canvass Committee met with the church collector before the third pledge year and reported that the family had never paid a cent on any of their pledges. Members were embarrassed and critical, but no one wanted to confront the family, so they agreed to accept the pledge and ignore it.

As the pledge campaign total was tallied for the annual meeting, the person who always canvassed the family felt haunted by a curiosity. She could not believe that this family had reneged on its promise. She knew that each year the congregation held an all-parish work weekend, and she learned that the family was always active in this work. These major projects ranged from painting to landscaping to refurbishing of the front steps. She also learned that when the volunteers showed up at the exterior painting project each morning, they saw the family's trucks, loaded with all the necessary equipment. The list included ladders in several sizes (including extension ladders reaching forty feet), electric sanders, scrapers, drop cloths, overalls for the volunteer painters, buckets with hooks, eight gallons of paint (tinted undercoat, oil-based, tinted top-coat, and latex), and professional brushes (Chinese horse hair for the undercoat, latex brushes for top-coat). The husband and wife supervised the volunteers for eight hours a day for two days.

The canvasser privately reported her findings to the treasurer, who responded, "Sure, they give. I sign their statement of time and material contribution each year for $500. It barely covers what they contribute." Next the canvasser sent the word around to the collector, the Board and the Finance Committee, who together responded, "Oh, well, that explains everything."

As we give and receive our offering, let us respect all the gifts that we bank on and cherish—gifts of time and talent as well as money.

THE MOMENT FOR KINDNESS

An old and anonymous offertory prelude reads, "If there is any kindness that I can show to any human being, let me do it now. Let me not defer it or neglect it, for I may not pass this way again." This may seem melodramatic for an offertory, but this potent saying opens deeper recesses of our experience and reveals times when we may have neglected acts of kindness, to a parent or to a stranger. It may prompt us to see how the timing of our gifts, no matter how small, can mean everything.

Once as I was driving around a Navajo reservation to explore key landmarks, I gave a lift to a couple of Navajos, shepherds by occupation, who had drunk their pockets empty in town off the reservation. I dropped them off at a little store near the head of the trail leading up to their mountain pasture. I had told them I was a pastor, and the man said he was a pastor too, but he had been "back-sliding for three years." As they got out of the car, the man said, "Can you spare five dollars?" I replied, "No. I do not think it would be right." The man said to me, "You'll probably need it later."

An hour later I parked my vehicle off Route 666 to wait out a massive hailstorm with deadly lightning. As the hailstones battered my roof and windows, I sat there and mulled over the morning's events. I knew that if I spent a week in the Navajo Nation I would not be uninvolved with Navajos, but at that moment I felt I had already given and done my part for the day. I was satisfied with myself.

After the storm I drove over the mesa to the extinct volcano magma called Shiprock and took some beautiful photographs. Then driving to Window Rock, I heard over KTNN Navajo radio an urgent appeal for anyone with information about a middle-aged white man wearing cut-off jeans to call the Navajo Police. It seemed that during that hailstorm, this man had picked up a teenage Navajo girl walking home after school and raped her.

A flash of memory hit me. It could have been the man I saw at breakfast earlier that week. He had sat at the table across from me in Taos, wore cutoff jeans, and was about thirty-five years old. He had smiled at me, though we did not exchange words.

Now I did nothing. After three more days of touring Anasazi ruins, I stopped for breakfast in Albuquerque before heading for California, and there was the man again sitting across from me and wearing cut-off jeans. Was he a rapist? He smiled.

I went into shock. Tension engulfed me about calling the police. I sensed it would be difficult to act in a way that would bring quick results. I might be wrong too.

And as I ate my scrambled eggs, I shrank from doing anything that would delay my itinerary.

My neglect since that morning has been my teacher. Toward the teenage Navajo girl, I did defer an act of kindness. And I did not pass that way again. We are humbled to know we may have only one moment for kindness in which to give or not give.

May the weekly offering remind us to be ever-ready for the opportunity for kindness.

APPEALS CAN BE MAJOR LEAGUE

ON ANY GIVEN SUNDAY in a congregation in central California, visitors may be surprised to hear a lay leader ask worshippers to give blood. This is earthquake country, and one way to get blood donations is to make the appeal in houses of worship.

On one Sunday while I was on sabbatical, my son and I attended this congregation's worship service, and in one morning we were asked for both blood donations and contributions for the church's annual pledge drive. Both campaigns were to start that day and extend through the following week. The presenters were excited, smiling, and quite confident, if appropriately awed by their tasks.

I felt put upon in no small way, and I turned to my son and said, "Is this heavy, or what?"

He nodded his head and smiled, "Sure, Dad. This is the Bay Area."

The service of worship had not even begun, and we had to sit in the pew and listen to this dire appeal in two parts for about ten minutes, five hundred pints of blood and five hundred pledges to raise five hundred thousand dollars.

As one way to cope with the stress I was feeling at that moment, I started to chuckle. I believed that I had come to worship with my son to seek sanctuary, to find healing from the poisons of the day, to strengthen the bond between us. I had to chuckle.

He looked over at me and said, "What's the problem, Dad? Listen, you're not back in the East where nothing ever happens without five days warning, like a hurricane or something. Earthquakes come at a moment's notice. You know how I got caught in the middle of the Santa Cruz–Aptos quake. You tried to reach me for a day or two, but I was all right. People take care of business out here."

"I was just thinking of the five hundred pledges for five hundred thou," I said, "on top of the blood drive. It's . . . oh, drop it."

I continued to chuckle and was almost unable to stop it from becoming a spasm of uncontrolled laughter. The more I thought of Eastern conservatism and formality, the more I wanted to laugh out loud. I was also laughing in joy about my son's maturity.

"Well, are you going to give to both?" I asked.

"Hardly. I would not choose this congregation," he replied. "It's your denomination. But I understand how they have the right idea." I saw he was not pleased with me.

The double appeal went against my minor-league Yankee grain of playing for small stakes in a climate of scarcity. That day I learned something that needs to be spread around. Religious congregations are often the major leagues. Members can't just be spectators; they are asked to play as well.

ACKNOWLEDGMENTS

The late Leonard Pierce of Fairhaven, Massachusetts, who belonged to the Unitarian Universalist Society of Fairhaven for more than fifty years, was an inspiration for many of these remarks. Leonard retired as the president of the National Bank at age fifty-five and took up volunteerism with a passion, lavishing his savings of time, talent, and money on the community where he had lived all his life. He once took me aside and shared this insight: "Bobby, the offering is the one place in the worship service where the people can make a difference. If we say we believe in our particular way of religion and we mean it, why not make the offering the center of the service? What I really mean is, I am proud to take the collection each Sunday, and I like to see the minister paid well, plus all the church staff."

Thanks are due also to the small urban congregation of the Universalist Unitarian Church of Brockton, Massachusetts. All of these offering remarks have been field-tested there.